I REPRESENT POSSIBILITIES

ONE MINUTE DEVOTIONAL

Cindy Miller-Wiley

DEDICATION	I
FORWARD	III
ABOUT THE AUTHOR	IV
GREATNESS WITHIN M.SPAEDER, PHYSICIAN ASSISTANT	1
ABE'S GAS STATION A MILLER	5
BOB'S PLACE B.MILLER	7
MAGGIE'S BEAUTY SALON M. SLADE	9
LUCY'S SOUP TRUCK (LUCY & RICK)	11
YOU REPRESENT POSSIBILITIES	13
FULL CIRCLE RADIO/BROADCASTING	15
OPPORTUNITY CONSTRUCTION C. PHINNEY	17
BARACK OBAMA	19
HAIR CARE T. MITCHELL	20
FINANCIAL CONSULTANT G. SWEET	21
CONNECTION	23
SAPPHIRE CLEANING CREW D. MAXWELL	24
IN THE BEGINNING PLACE J. PHINNEY	26
GOD'S HELPING HAND Y. CHISHOLM	27
PRAISE, WORSHIP AND ADORATION C. HAWKINS	29
I AM WHO I AM	31
SPARKLE FOUNDATION S. BICKLES	32
DELECTABLE DELIGHTS D.CRUZ-NEAL	34
NEED A TAXI OBI	36
SONGS OF PRAISE V. LAWSON	38
BARNABAS T. SWEET	39
KINGDOM CULTURE DESIGNS B. LINDER	41
EDUCATOR B.J. MORTON.	43
DETERMINATION S. EVANS	44
THE BEC PLEX BY KEN K. GAINES	46
SPA THERAPY STUDIO A. ASH-MILLER	48

Dedication

This book is dedicated to all who know they have God-given possibilities and what they need to do next is the "work."

Inside each of us are the gifts and talents that God gave us before we were in our mother's womb.

Now is the time to get the work done and bring those possibilities to 'life' and 'victory.'

The possibilities are beyond your wildest imagination

If you dare to believe.

The possibilities you can share with others will open gates you will go through that you thought could never happen. But God!

Tap into those possibilities today and begin again. Let God lead you. Listen for his prompting through the Holy Spirit.

Who would have thought I would be an international author? My book 'Life After the Diagnosis' was showcased at the London Book Fair, Frankfurt Germany Book Fair, and the LA Times Festival of Books.

I survived gastric cancer, hyperthyroidism, and two car accidents that could have taken my life. Yet I'm still here pursuing my dream.

See what the Lord has done in and for me.

Forward

Welcome to "I Represent Possibilities"

These devotional snippets represent encouragement & inspiration on a daily basis as a reminder of the possibilities within you.

The Bible says that we should not 'despise these small beginnings for the Lord rejoices to see the work begin' - **Zechariah 4:10.'**

Though thy beginning was small, yet thy latter end should greatly increase. - **Job 8**:7.

Take the time to listen to that still, small voice pushing you into your purpose and your destiny.

A little one shall become a thousand, and a small one a strong nation: I, the Lord, will hasten it in his time. - **Isaiah 60:22.**

About the Author

Cindy was born to the late George W. and Edith I. Miller. She is the youngest of 12 siblings, with only one sister still living.

She has been writing since she was 10 years old when she won her first school competition.

Cindy is the proud mother of one daughter, Dawn, and has three grandchildren Deija, Des'ree, and Devon. Her great-grandchildren are Nyi, Raylynn, Raelle, Reign, and Rue.

Cindy stated that she writes under the guidance of the Holy Spirit, not man. She believes that the greatest gift God has given her is the inspiration and encouragement to write for others.

She loves to travel and can't wait to go on a book tour.

Cindy considers herself blessed to be a blessing.

Cindy showcased her book, Life After the Diagnosis, last year in London, Frankfurt, Germany, and at the LA Book Festival.

I Represent Possibilities is her latest book.

GREATNESS WITHIN
M.Spaeder, Physician Assistant

'I did not know I could change the world until I did.'

Greatness is within us all. We just have to figure out what our superpower is and how we are supposed to use that gift to better the world. (Possibilities)

Greatness begins by believing that you have a purpose in life. Then, following that purpose, avoiding distractions along the way until you have achieved your goal.

Just by reaching your goal, you have achieved greatness. How great it is depends on how big your dream is.

My greatness was achieved by realizing that what I thought was my path in life was not what I thought it would be. By changing course from being a destructive force to a healer. Both to the world and myself.

Achieving greatness is a winding road. Believe in yourself and follow the leading of the Holy Spirit.

Remember, greatness is in you. You must follow your path and believe you are greater than you think.

IMPORTANT MESSAGE

JUNE, 2024

2,508 STUDENTS GRADUATED FROM
HOWARD UNIVERSITY
'LARGEST CLASS IN 157 YEARS'

POSSIBILITIES

The Lord says, "I will guide you along the best pathway for your life. I will advise you and watch over you." - Psalm 32:8

For we are His workmanship, created in Christ Jesus for good works which God prepared beforehand that we should walk in them. - Ephesians 2:10

Abe's Gas Station
A Miller

He was young, but the possibility within him was to own his own business.

He worked at the Steelton branch of Harrisburg Steel Mill for several years, but his ambition was to own a business.

One day, on his way home from work, he spotted a gas station that was up for sale. He spoke to his Dad about it and decided he would try to buy it. He accomplished that.

It was the first black-owned gas station in Harrisburg on 11th & Herr Streets.

He then moved to California, where he was in an accident that left him paralyzed. The possibility of his success was that he continued to do the work and started a business that instructed clients on how to fix their cars.

Are you looking to start a business? Do your research, engage others who are like-minded, and show what possibilities can do, especially through Christ.

With men, this is impossible, but with God, all things are possible. Matthew - 19:26

Bob's Place
B.Miller

For many years, he had dabbled at doing different businesses.

One day, he saw a bowling alley for sale. He inquired and was able to purchase the bowling alley to help get the kids off the street.

The possibility within him didn't stop there. Although he didn't outwardly say that it was because of God, he expressed it in private and also bought a laundry mat to help the community and a truck that he turned into a salad truck at the Kipona.

The possibilities within him led to victories in many areas, and the community was blessed.

Dream big. Anything is possible if you do the work.

God is for you.

Maggie's Beauty Salon
M. Slade

She was employed by the then Harrisburg State Hospital. She was the first black beautician employed there.

In addition to working at the State Hospital, she had her own business in her home. Maggie's Beauty Salon. She was proud of all she had accomplished and raising her granddaughter.

The possibilities for her were endless as she pursued all that was within her. God blessed her and her hands.

Her name is Maggie Slade, and she is victorious till her death.

Got a dream? Never give up on it. God is with you and for you.

If you can believe, all things are possible to him who believes. - Mark 9:23

Lucy's Soup Truck
(Lucy & Rick)

There is a woman named Lucy who wanted to feed the homeless. She prayed and asked God for direction. She started doing the work, and all the possibilities God had placed inside of her began to come to fruition.

She and her husband joined forces with another couple who fed the homeless like iron sharpens iron and began to feed on the 3rd Saturday of each month. She needed a larger vehicle to distribute more items. God took care of that. Food led to clothing, tents, shoes, and so much more. What a blessing.

When you tap into, I represent possibilities; you give God an opportunity to do His thing. He wants praise, glory, and honor. So, He will show up and show out so that all will know it was Him.

You represent possibilities for others to see what can be done when you trust and believe, as Lucy and her husband did.

She and her husband represent possibilities.

How about you?

I Represent Possibilities
By Cindy Miller-Wiley

YOU REPRESENT POSSIBILITIES

You represent possibilities

Is what the Spirit spoke to me

You represent everything is possible

When you trust God

He'll help you to achieve

All that He has planned from

Womb to birth and so much more

Were created as possibilities

When you trust God

As He opens many doors.

The word says nothing is impossible

If you only believe

The time is now for your possibilities

For victory is yours

Get ready to receive.

I REPRESENT POSSIBILITIES
BY CINDY MILLER-WILEY

Full Circle Radio/Broadcasting

A group of talented, gifted men (Used to be Me & Us) waited 52 years for their dreams of having a recording studio, radio, art entertainment, and so much more. They were waiting for the possibility to come to fruition and to come together in victory.

It happened as of May 2024

God had not forgotten the promises He made them, and they stayed the course until it was their time.

All I can say is, 'Won't He Do It'. When He places a possibility in your spirit, He never leaves you. When you keep Him first, He'll make sure that all that you've prayed for will come to pass.

What a wonderful feeling to know when you've prayed, cried, and toiled for many years to have your dream finally come true.

He's a wonderful, on-time God. The possibilities have been with them all these years, and He says, 'Now is the time.'

Stop and check out Full Circle Entertainment. You won't be disappointed.

Congratulations, men, for staying the course

I REPRESENT POSSIBILITIES
BY CINDY MILLER-WILEY

Opportunity Construction
C. Phinney

There is a young man who had a dream of owning his own construction company. He had worked construction for the state of Pennsylvania for many years and felt he could do so much more. He strived to help others learn the trade and how they could do great things with their lives based on his experience and training them.

The possibility of getting grants and hiring staff extending into a non-profit for a men's and women's shelter was beyond his greatest expectations.

The possibilities are within you because God gave them to you. You are never to forget what He has done, and you encourage others to fulfill their dreams and their God-given gifts and talents. Most of all, never give up.

We are all born with the possibility to show to the world so that our God gets praise, glory, and honor.

We are blessed to be a blessing. He could employ several people who wouldn't have had a chance at employment. But To God Be The Glory!

I Represent Possibilities
By Cindy Miller-Wiley

Barack Obama

In 2004, a man from Chicago, Illinois, dared to believe that he could become the first African American president of the United States.

The possibilities were endless for his path. God had gifted him for our nation at such a time.

He shook up America when he made the announcement, and all white and black Americans were looking for change. He was the change.

God had prepared him with all the possibilities inside of him to do what he did for 2 presidential terms. What a victory for him and for our people. Hope came alive again.

Possibilities….work it. It's in you.

Hair Care

T. Mitchell

She has worked at many salons as an employee and assistant manager but not as a manager.

The possibilities God placed within her were to take her from where she was to where she is today. She is the manager of a major salon (Hair Cuttery), and over 15+ employees report to her.

She can now teach and instruct new employees in customer service and how to move when the time is right into their God-given possibilities.

Financial Consultant
G. Sweet

She has always had an interest in finance, from her assignment working in another church to the administrator in her current position. She oversees the finances of the church under the leadership of the Pastor. God knew the possibilities he had placed in her.

She took her experience as a bookkeeper to another level of possibilities when she was asked to become the financial consultant for a construction company and many other businesses and churches that needed her services.

The possibility of teaching others about finances and getting out of debt was another area when God gave her another assignment to perform. He can take little and make it much when it's in His hands. She is also a Notary Public.

She is an asset to the body of Christ.

I REPRESENT POSSIBILITIES
BY CINDY MILLER-WILEY

CONNECTION

Connect with like-minded people. God has blessed them, and they did the work. They trusted and believed that all things are possible if you only believe.

He's waiting for you. He already knows what He's put in you. Do you know? The possibilities are endless.

Trust Him

Sapphire Cleaning Crew
D. Maxwell

She is an entrepreneur and there was more in store for her.

The possibilities have always been in her. She just had to wait upon the Lord. She attempted other business ventures, but it wasn't the time. God's timing is always perfect.

She did just that when she joined forces with her cleaning partner, who established Sapphire Cleaning Crew.

God had been speaking to her the whole time when he told her the possibilities are endless within you because I put them there.

She applied for a cleaning contract at Hoffman Ford. One of the largest automobile dealerships in the area. They won the contract for $50,000.

The possibilities are endless when you let God lead and direct you. Just do the work and watch Him work.

I Represent Possibilities
By Cindy Miller Wiley

In The Beginning Place

J. Phinney

She had a desire to start a daycare center based on the possibilities God had placed in her.

She spoke with the Pastor of her church, and they opened up classes in the church in 2018.

She and her staff touched many lives until she decided to move the business to York and work on her degree. She's still in the process as God continues to push her into her destiny and all the possibilities within her.

God's Helping Hand
Y. Chisholm

I met her approximately 13 years ago.

She was a CNA working at a facility, and I was the Director of the Memory Care Unit.

I saw then, as I've seen over the years, her commitment to her patients and her passion to make things better for them.

She realized that she was on a journey of all the possibilities God had placed in her.

Several years ago, she started her own business, and it has been shining ever since. She took on a big responsibility while still supporting her family and moved to another city. She did it.

I am so proud of her and all that she has done and all that she is going to do for the cause of Christ.

I REPRESENT POSSIBILITIES
BY CINDY MILLER-WILEY

Praise, Worship and Adoration
C. Hawkins

Her name is Cheryl, and the possibilities God has given her are beyond, beyond.

She began playing the piano many, many years ago, which elevated her to an organ and sound keyboard.

She plays from the depths of her soul as she ministers at her church and at any event where she is showcased.

She gives all glory and honor to the Almighty God and how He has used her for His service.

She is getting ready for her next possibility of recording a CD. We wait with great anticipation, expecting God to show up and show His glory when it is released.

She also has a holistic healthcare business.

I REPRESENT POSSIBILITIES
BY CINDY MILLER-WILEY

I am who I am

LeBron James, with no father, no college education, no training, and very few role models except his single mother, Gloria, handed him young, dirt poor, and black $420,000 per week at the age of 18 to play basketball and become the face of the $75 billion NBA.

Do you see the possibilities within him?

Could that be you?

(Excerpt from Evita Ellis)

Sparkle Foundation
S. Bickles

She has been grieving since her daughter passed away, but she knew that there was more for her to do.

The possibilities within her drove her to create a foundation in memory of her daughter Tawanna.

She gathers toys, clothing, and other items to send back to her home for the children there. She comes from Ghana.

She shares with us that each time she goes home, all their happy faces and their receptive response will take your breath away.

When God places something in your spirit to do for the kingdom, do it. He chose you.

She also has a jewelry business.

The possibilities are endless.

I REPRESENT POSSIBILITIES
BY CINDY MILLER-WILEY

Delectable Delights
D.Cruz-Neal

She was only 12 years old when she talked with her grandmother about making sticky buns. How excited she was when she brought them to her church as a test kitchen, which went over hand over fist.

From there, God took her to another level. She began making chocolate chip cookies. Then she moved again to oatmeal raisin and sugar cookies. My God, how exciting.

To be so young, the possibilities within her have been beyond her wildest imagination as she put her business in the master's hand.

She is now 17 and looking at the possibilities God is speaking to her spirit.

We acknowledge her and the up-and-coming youth as they begin to start their own businesses. They need our encouragement and support.

God is faithful and will be with you every step of the way.

The possibilities rest within you.

Commit to the Lord whatever you do

And He will establish your plans. - Proverbs 16:3

Need A Taxi
Obi

He came from Nigeria many years ago and became a citizen of the United States.

He started out driving a taxi, but he knew the possibilities that God had put in him would evolve into a taxi business of his own.

He helped to support two daughters who are doctors and have returned to their home in Nigeria.

He has another daughter and son who live in Pennsylvania and Virginia. Both are pursuing additional education.

His clients love and respect him and the advice he gives them. He is a major prayer warrior and intercessor.

He travels back to his home country when He gets the opportunity. His wife is still there, hoping that they will all be together one day.

God said,

"My presence will go with you.

I'll see the journey to the end". - Exodus 33:13

Songs of Praise
V. Lawson

Whatever possibilities God has placed in your spirit, just do the work.

She is an educator and gives God praise and worship through her voice as she lifts songs of praise and adoration to Him.

What a prayer warrior and blessing she is to the Kingdom as she continues her journey.

Can't nobody do you like Jesus!!

Barnabas

T. Sweet

There aren't many people who don't know him and his attitude and delivery of encouragement.

He can meet someone in a grocery store, parking lot, or on the corner and will listen and give them a word of encouragement.

The possibilities within him speak for itself. He is always blessing someone at his church, their children, those starting new businesses, and so much more.

When was the last time you paid it forward for all that God has done for you?

The return can't be measured.

Through the ministry, he supports two African countries and supports other ministries in the area.

Donating doesn't always mean money. Your time in helping someone else move forward is your greatest reward.

He's the PASTOR

Whoever dwells in the shelter of the Most High

Will rest in the shadow of the Almighty. - Psalm 91:1

Kingdom Culture Designs
B. Linder

He had been praying about a tee shirt business when he received God's blessing to start.

He realized that there were other possibilities within him, which was and always had been music. He started a record company, Let Go – Let God, under the unction of the Holy Spirit, and God continues to use him and his team on their journey for the cause of Christ.

Devote yourselves to prayer with an alert mind and a thankful heart. - Col. 4:2

Educator
B.J. Morton.

She is a single mother of 4 children 3 have already graduated from college, and one more since graduation this year, deciding on his next move.

All her life, she wanted to be a teacher. She graduated from Harrisburg Community College, Penn State University, and Scranton University. Nothing is impossible when your hand is in the hands of the Almighty.

She has a double master's degree. How awesome is our God? There are so many possibilities within her, and see what the Lord has done.

All the possibilities manifested!

Determination

S. Evans

She was determined that cancer nor the dark part of her life was going to deter her from serving the Lord. – She has testified about this many times.

That was her past, but Christ was her future

When he called her into evangelism, it was a God send.

Serving Christ doesn't come without highs and lows

You just can't stay there when it's negative.

You must rise above like the phoenix and let the ashes become a garment of praise.

Let the possibilities in Christ push you to your purpose and destiny in him.

What are your possibilities?

I REPRESENT POSSIBILITIES
BY CINDY MILLER-WILEY

THE BEC PLEX

Ken is the owner/operator of THE BEC PLEX Advertising and originates from Harrisburg PA before moving to Augusta, GA. He is currently involved in advertising.

His God-given possibilities has provided opportunities in broadcasting, education, and radio.

He has been in business for over 15+ years. His building has sponsored concerts with up-and-coming stars, gospel fest, and many other entertainment venues.

Ken knew from a young age that he would be in the entertainment business, and God utilized the possibilities within him to push him to his purpose and destiny.

He is on the move for the cause of Christ.

Ken is married with 2 children.

I REPRESENT POSSIBILITIES
BY CINDY MILLER WILEY

Spa Therapy Studio
A. Ash-Miller

Alana is the Owner and Operator of Spa Therapy in Charlotte, North Carolina

Alana has been in business for over 15+ years, and God has used her God-given possibilities to touch people's lives all over North Carolina.

Alana is married and has 2 children.

She is blessed in all she does for the kingdom and the cause of Christ. The possibilities within her were beyond her wildest imagination.

Alana originates from Harrisburg PA before moving to Charlotte NC. She is a massage therapist and with her God-given possibilities owns and operates SPA Therapy.

I REPRESENT POSSIBILITIES
BY CINDY MILLER-WILEY

9 798330 475919